Duane Barnhart's

CARTOONING BASICS

CREATING THE CHARACTERS

written and illustrated by

Duane Barnhart

co-author, Angie Barnhart

Fourth Edition
Completely Revised

Cartoon Connections Press • White Bear Lake, Minnesota

Dedication

*Cartooning Basics is dedicated to our daughters,p
Katie, Amy, Angela, April, Danelle, Deanna, Holly.*

*And for
Joshua, Elliott, Lucas, Noah, Corbin,
Emma, Aidan, Hannah, Isaac, Jeremiah.*

*And for
Future 'Grandcartoonists'.*

Thanks to the many people who helped make this book possible:

To the thousands of students and teachers who have invited us to share these cartooning ideas and techniques in their classrooms.

To schools, arts organizations and Parent/Teacher Organizations who work effortlessly to support art in schools for children in spite of funding difficulties.

To the O'Gara Family for their help and support.

To Jody Karlen for her close attention to detail and finding all of our speling misteaks.

To Shawn Gritzmacher for his photo support.

To Dave Mruz for encouragement, expertise and friendship.

Cartooning Basics – Creating The Characters

Written and illustrated by Duane Barnhart
Co-authored by Angie Barnhart

©Copyright 1997, 1998, 2003, 2004
Cartoon Connections Press
Published and Distributed by Cartoon Connections Press
P.O. Box 10889, White Bear Lake, MN 55110
www.CartooningBasics.com

First Printing: 1997
Second Printing: 1998
Third Printing: 2003
Fourth Printing: 2004, completely revised

Library of Congress Control Number: 2004094645

ISBN: 0-9657136-4-4

Cartooning Basics is proudly printed in the United States of America.

CONTENTS

In Memory of Charles M. Schulz

Foreword by Jim Davis

About the authors and what's new

In Memory

of Charles M. Schulz

We can't imagine life without the 'Peanuts' gang. Charlie Brown, Lucy, Linus, Snoopy, Woodstock and all the rest have become icons for our own 'humanness'. We are thankful to the Charles M. Schulz family for keeping his memory alive at the Schulz Museum and in comic strip 'reruns.' Now, even after his death, young cartoon fans can still enjoy his pure, understated wit through these time-less, simple, yet, complex characters.

We are proud to have been a part of the St. Paul, Minnesota's 'Peanuts Paintoff' events for the last few years creating statues depicting the 'Peanuts' characters. We can think of no better way to honor Minnesota's most loved and famous cartoonist, Charles 'Sparky' Schulz. Many thanks to the O'Gara family for sponsoring our part in this wonderful and fun-filled event!

Sparky, life goes on without you, but it's not quite the same. You inspired us and encouraged us to teach, and thrill, thousands of young cartoonists with the how-to knowledge of drawing their own cartoons. We can never thank you enough!

Duane and Angie Barnhart

1997

"Probably one of the best things about Duane Barnhart's book is his emphasis upon the fun and joy of cartooning. I don't think anyone can deny that there are times when it is extremely hard work and takes total dedication. I do believe, however, that drawing funny pictures, whether for newspapers or simply on a letter to a friend, can be wonderfully satisfying. Duane Barnhart leads you, in his writing and cartoon samples, to the sort of start that everyone, who wishes to draw cartoons, certainly needs."

Charles M. Schulz
Creator of Peanuts
1922 - 2000

Foreword

by Jim Davis

Well, this is just great. After years of struggling to figure out how to draw hands and feet, Duane Barnhart comes out with *Cartooning Basics* and makes it all look easy! Where were you back in the '70s when I was trying to get syndicated, Duane?

Cartooning Basics is an entertaining read and a wonderful how-to for the beginning cartoonist or for anyone who wants to improve their drawing skills.

Years before I considered cartooning as a vocation, I cartooned to express myself, and, to make my mom laugh (she was always an easy mark). As with anything, the better you become at something, the more you enjoy it.

What are you waiting for? Grab your paper and pencil and start having some fun!

ABOUT THE AUTHORS

Duane Barnhart has taught his successful cartooning techniques to tens of thousands of enthusiastic students in schools, libraries and art centers in assembly programs and as an artist-in-residence. Duane has been an inspiration to thousands of aspiring young cartoonists.

His experiences in teaching students inspired him to write *Cartooning Basics* in 1997. Since that time the book has won several awards and been translated into Chinese and Spanish.

As a professional cartoonist, Duane has been published in regional and national magazines including *The Saturday Evening Post*, *MPLS St. Paul Magazine*, the *Lake Country Journal* and *Cabin Life*. Duane has drawn a nationally syndicated cartoon strip, several advertising comic books, designed many products using licensed Warner Brothers and Disney Characters. He has illustrated many children's books and text books.

Co-author/editor **Angie Barnhart** is a commercial artist, designer, and art director. She uses her cartooning and illustrating skills to produce printed publications for businesses and publishers. Angie has extensive experience conducting cartooning residencies and school visits working with elementary and middle school students. She has taught cartooning in schools, art centers, libraries and college youth programs for over ten years.

Duane and Angie enjoy teaching cartooning to young people each year in their residences, school and library visits. Together, they manage and operate Cartoon Connections. When not cartooning they enjoy their cabin, seven daughters, ten grandchildren, old cat and a rotund, but devoted, dog!

HERE'S WHAT'S NEW IN THIS COMPLETELY REVISED EDITION OF CARTOONING BASICS!

 Over 400 additional illustrations!!

 Difficulty levels for each lesson

 Not very complex
Zoom on through!

 A little more difficult.
Slow down.

 More challenging.
Take your time.

Use these icons as reference only! Challenge yourself as your skills improve.

 More lessons and examples
New and easier ways to draw bodies for beginning cartoonists and expanded sections covering expression and head accessories.

 Create animation, panel cartoons, getting ideas and a lot more!
Try these animation and comic strip lessons for a practical application for your newly created cartoon characters!

 Flip book animations in the margins
Flip the edges of the book. for some entertaining animation fun. They might give you a few ideas for your own animation!

INTRODUCING NO. 2 AND CARTOONING BASICS!

WELCOME TO CARTOONING BASICS!

CREATING CHARACTERS!!

MY NAME IS NUMBER 2.

IN CASE YOU HAVEN'T GUESSED, I'M A NO. 2 PENCIL AND I'M GOING TO EXPLAIN THE TECHNIQUES AND EXERCISES IN THIS BOOK.

SOME LESSONS ARE EASY!

AND OTHERS MAY BE MORE CHALLENGING.

BUT ALL OF THE LESSONS ARE FUN!

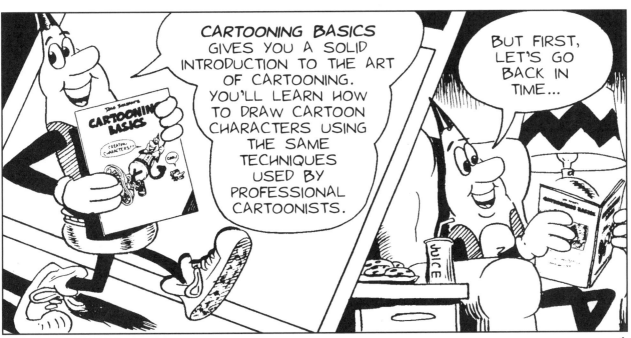

CARTOONING BASICS GIVES YOU A SOLID INTRODUCTION TO THE ART OF CARTOONING. YOU'LL LEARN HOW TO DRAW CARTOON CHARACTERS USING THE SAME TECHNIQUES USED BY PROFESSIONAL CARTOONISTS.

BUT FIRST, LET'S GO BACK IN TIME...

A BIT OF CARTOONING HISTORY!

Cartoons have been around a very long time. Some artists who painted in caves over 20,000 years ago tried to show movement in their animals by drawing repeated patterns of leg movements. Was this the first attempt at animation?

Editorial cartoonist, **Thomas Nast** created the elephant and donkey symbols for the American Republican and Democratic political parties. Nast even drew cartoons of Santa Claus. He lived in the 1800's when Abraham Lincoln was President of the United States.

Some say that the word 'cartoon' comes from the Italian word **cartone'** which means CARTON. Artists sketched on inexpensive carton material. These rough drawings became known as cartones. These eventually became known as *cartoons*.

The first newspaper comic strip appeared in the **New York World** in May, 1895. **Hogan's Alley** starred the **Yellow Kid** by **Richard Outcault**. The public *loved* it! It was created to entertain *and* sell newspapers. The term "Yellow Journalism" came from this cartoon strip.

Among many other talents, **Benjamin Franklin** was a cartoonist. He drew this cartoon way back in 1754 to unify the American Colonies. This is known as an editorial cartoon. Editorial cartoons are still enjoyed today.

The first animated movie was made by **James Stewart Blackton** in 1906. It was called **Humorous Phases of Funny Faces**. He used a new fangled invention made by **Thomas Edison** - the movie projector.

FIND OUT MORE AT THE LIBRARY!

1914

The first animated dinosaur was *Gertie the Dinosaur*, drawn by **Windsor McKay** in 1914. Mr. McKay drew thousands of pictures of Gertie, then showed them all very rapidly on a movie projector to make her move! She was the talk of the town!

IT'S A *BIRD*, IT'S A PLANE, IT'S . . .
ZOOM!
SUPERMAN!
1938

The first comic book, published in 1933, was called *Funnies on Parade.* It reprinted popular newspaper comic strips. In 1938, *Action Comics,* issue #1, was published with its own character and its own story. That character was none other than *SUPERMAN!*

LET'S CALL HIM MORTIMER.
Cartoonist
I LIKE MICKEY MOUSE BETTER!
1928

Only a few years after *Gertie,* young cartoonist **Walt Disney** tried his hand at producing his own animated films. In 1928, he and his animator friend, **Ub Iwerks**, created the world's first talking mouse. Since then, Disney Studios has grown into an animation empire. Mrs. Disney chose Mickey's now famous name.

GOOD NIGHT, SNOOPY.
GOOD NIGHT, CHARLIE BROWN.
1969

Snoopy and **Charlie Brown** went around the moon in 1969! During this Apollo 10 NASA Space Mission, the command module was named *Charlie Brown,* and the lunar module was called *Snoopy.* **Charles M. Schulz**, creator of the *Peanuts* gang, stayed on earth.

ZOOM!
COMIC BOOKS!
1930

Felix the Cat, created by **Pat Sullivan** in 1917, became the first cartoon on television in 1930. Felix appeared in newspaper comic strip in 1923. Many characters, like Felix, have been in movies, television, comic strips, video games and, of course, COMIC BOOKS!

1978

In the 1950's, young **Jim Davis** had asthma. While recuperating, he practiced his drawing skills. He lived on a farm with *25 cats*! In 1978, he used his drawing skills and knowledge of all those crazy cats to create *GARFIELD,* the world's most famous cartoon cat!

3

LET'S GET STARTED!

FIRST OF ALL, FIND A COMFORTABLE PLACE TO DRAW!

SOME CARTOONISTS NEED PEACE AND QUIET.

DO NOT DISTURB!
GO AWAY!
SCRAM

Others can cartoon just about anywhere! But wherever you decide is best for you …

DRAW EVERY DAY!
BE PATIENT
YOU CAN DO IT!
MAKE IT FUN!

… a flat surface and good lighting are a good idea! Next, you've got to have the **right stuff**!

HAVE YOUR BASIC CARTOONING KIT HANDY!

Mechanical pencils are great for math but <u>not</u> for drawing cartoons. Use a good, old fashioned Number 2 pencil like the pros do.

No. 2 pencils

soft erasers

Black inking pens– fine or medium point

MY 'TOONS

Plain **two-pocket folder** to decorate and hold your 'toons

IDEAS!

Folder or envelope to hold reference pictures

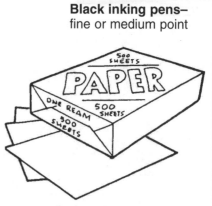

PAPER
500 SHEETS

Plain White Paper copier or computer paper

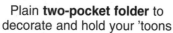

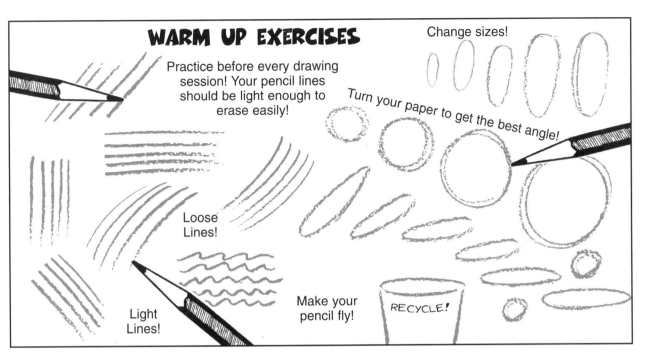

WARM UP EXERCISES

Practice before every drawing session! Your pencil lines should be light enough to erase easily!

Change sizes!

Turn your paper to get the best angle!

Loose Lines!

Light Lines!

Make your pencil fly!

RECYCLE!

WE'RE HEADED IN THE RIGHT DIRECTION!

WHEN YOU'RE JUST STARTING TO DRAW THE HUMAN HEAD, AN EGG SHAPE OR OVAL IS A GOOD BEGINNING PLACE.

LATER YOU'LL GET MORE ADVENTUROUS WITH HEAD SHAPES.

WHAT ARE WE WAITING FOR? LET'S DRAW SOME COOL, CARTOON HUMAN HEADS!!!

LET'S DRAW A HEAD WITH THE EYES IN THE MIDDLE!

DIFFICULTY LEVEL

Guidelines go half way up and half way across.

Nose and mouth line.

Eye line.

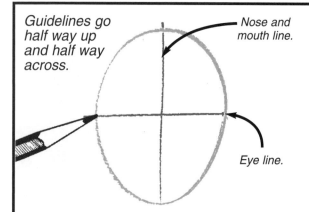

1. Draw an oval using a *light* pencil line. Next, add guidelines like this.

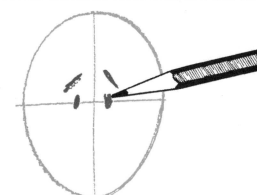

2. Now draw the eyes on the eye line.

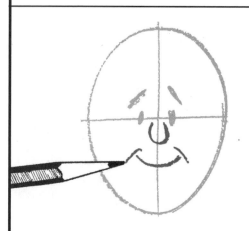

3. The nose and a mouth are centered on the vertical line.

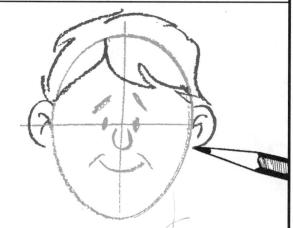

4. Add hair and ears. Ears go at each end of the eye line.

See pages 22-26 for more expressions, eyes, noses, ears and head accessories.

5. Trace the lines you want to save with a black pen and erase all pencil lines.

6. With a few additions and small changes, you can create a whole new character!

IDEAS FOR HEADS WITH A MIDDLE EYE LINE

Check out pages 22-26 for more expressions and head accessory ideas.

DIFFICULTY LEVEL

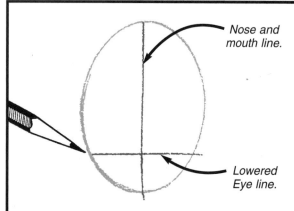

Nose and mouth line.

Lowered Eye line.

1. Draw the guidelines *lightly* with your pencil. Draw the eye line close to the bottom.

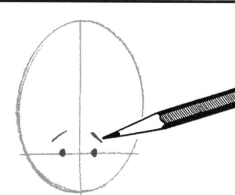

2. Draw the eyes on the eye line. Add eyebrows.

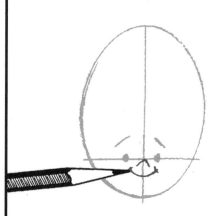

3. Add a small nose and mouth centered on the vertical line.

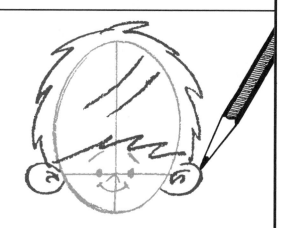

4. Add hair and ears.

Lowering the eye line doesn't always result in a younger character, but it's a good way to do it.

Try a lower eye line and use a BIG nose to see what happens!

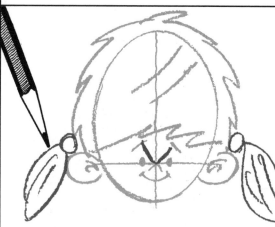

5. Hair style can change this character into a girl. A letter 'V' between the eyes shows mischief.

6. Trace in ink and erase the pencil lines.

IDEAS FOR HEADS WITH A LOWER EYE LINE

Check out pages 22-23 for more expression ideas.

RAISE THE EYE LINE FOR OLDER CHARACTERS

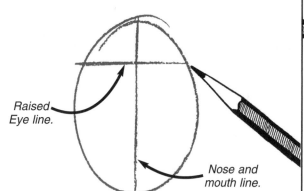

Raised Eye line.

Nose and mouth line.

1. Again, we start with a *light* oval and draw the guidelines. Notice the raised eyeline.

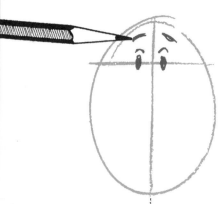

2. Add the eyes on the eye line, one on either side of the vertical line.

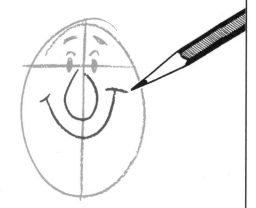

3. Draw the nose and mouth centered on the vertical line.

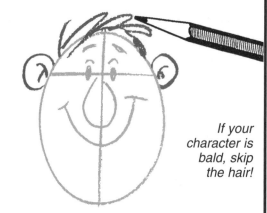

If your character is bald, skip the hair!

4. Add ears at the ends on the eye line, then add some hair.

Larger noses will help your character look older.

5. Trace your character in black ink and erase all pencil lines!

With a few extras, you can create a really wacky looking guy! Use your great imagination!

IDEAS FOR HEADS WITH A RAISED EYE LINE

Check out pages 22-26 for more expressions and additions.

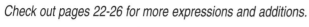

DIFFICULTY LEVEL

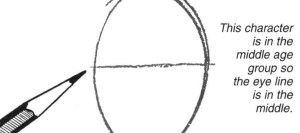

This character is in the middle age group so the eye line is in the middle.

1. Draw the head shape. Add the eye line at the top, middle or bottom of the head – where ever you want.

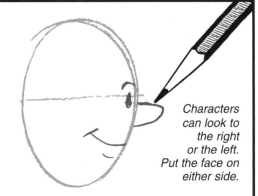

Characters can look to the right or the left. Put the face on either side.

2. Add one eye on the eye line near the edge of the head shape. Add the nose, like this, and a mouth.

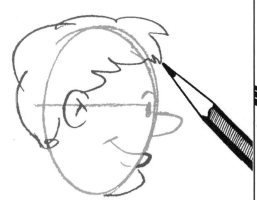

3. Add the ear inside the oval on the eye line. Add a lip, chin and hair style.

4. Trace with your ink pen and erase all pencil lines.

6. Add a few extras and you can create a new character! See page 26 for more ideas.

THE SIDE VIEW WORKS FOR ALL DIFFERENT CHARACTERS!

IDEAS FOR CREATING PROFILES

Eye line is closer to the bottom.

Eye line is closer to the middle.

Eye line is closer to the top.

HEADS TURNING SLIGHTLY IS CALLED A 3/4 OR ANGLED VIEW

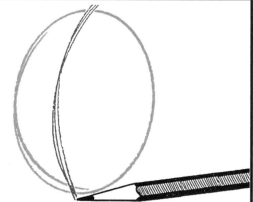

1. Make the head shape with your *light* pencil lines as usual.

2. Choose which way your character's head will turn and *lightly* draw a curved line from top to bottom.

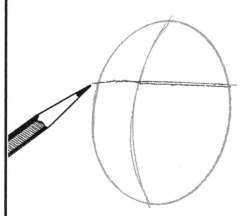

3. Choose the age of your character and draw the eye line. Your line may be at the top, middle, or bottom.

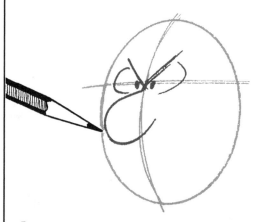

4. Eyes go next to the curved line and the nose points in the direction that the character is looking.

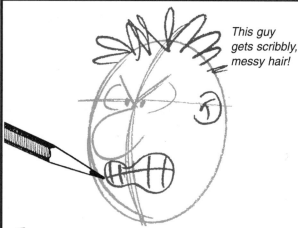

This guy gets scribbly, messy hair!

5. Draw the ear on the eye line and inside the head shape. Add the mouth and hair.

Chins and jaws can make your character a real individual. Go ahead and modify them.

6. Trace the lines you want to keep with your black pen. Erase all the pencil lines.

IDEAS FOR TURNING HEADS

Notice the position of the eye line in the different characters.

Eye line is closer to the bottom.

Eye line is close to the middle.

Eye line is closer to the top.

Notice the position of the eye line for the different characters.

CHARACTERS CAN LOOK UP. . . JUST CURVE THE EYE LINE.

AS YOU LOOK AT OUR EGG-SHAPED HEAD FROM THE END, YOU SEE A CIRCLE SHAPE, SO LET'S USE A CIRCLE TO DRAW HEADS LOOKING UP AND LOOKING DOWN!

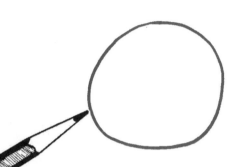

1. Create a circle, which will be the bottom of the character's head, with *light* pencil line.

2. Draw the vertical line. Curve the eye line as shown.

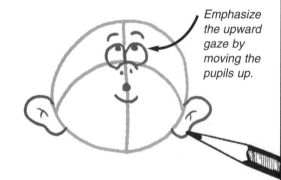

Emphasize the upward gaze by moving the pupils up.

3. Add the eyes on the eye line. Add the nose and mouth centered on the vertical line and ears at the ends of the eye line.

4. Add hair and any final details.

5. Trace with black pen and erase your *light* pencil lines. Things are looking up!

THEY CAN LOOK DOWN. CURVE THE EYE LINE THE OTHER WAY.

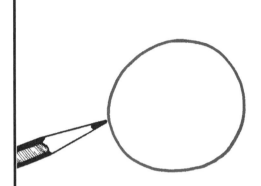

1. Make the circular head shape for the top of the head with *light* pencil line.

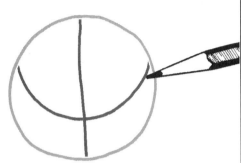

2. Draw the vertical line. Curve the eye line as shown for a character looking down.

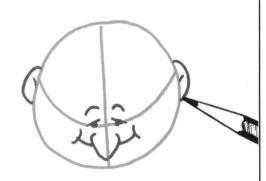

3. Add the eyes on the eye line. Add the nose and mouth centered on the vertical line and ears at the ends of the eye line.

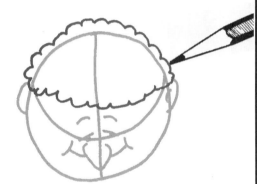

4. Add hair and any final details.

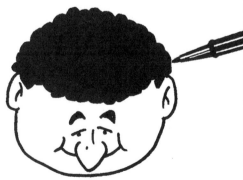

5. Trace with black pen and erase *light* pencil lines. What's he looking at?

ENJOY THE VIEW! UP OR DOWN, IT'S GOOD TO KNOW HOW TO DRAW YOUR CHARACTERS LOOKING AT THE FLOOR OR WAY UP TO THE SKY!

CHARACTERS CAN LOOK UP, DOWN AND ALL AROUND!

IDEAS FOR MORE CHARACTERS WITH DIFFERENT SHAPED HEADS

Notice some of these heads are created using multiple shapes. Experiment with many different combined shapes to see how many new and fun head shapes you can create.

MODIFY THE EXPRESSION OF YOUR CHARACTERS!

Different expressions will help your character tell its own cartoon story!

IDEAS FOR DRAWING EXPRESSIONS

Don't forget to add noses and ears! See pages 24 and 25.

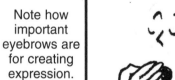 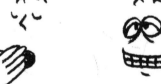 

MIX AND MATCH EYES AND MOUTHS FOR EVEN MORE CARTOON FUN !

EYES AND NOSES FOR YOUR CHARACTERS

Notice how some of these noses resemble letters of the alphabet? You can stretch those letters, pull them, turn them backwards and upside down until they look like a great cartoon nose.

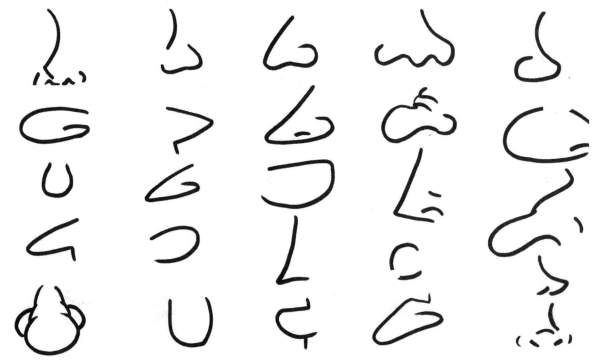

EAR AND MOUTH SHAPES TO USE

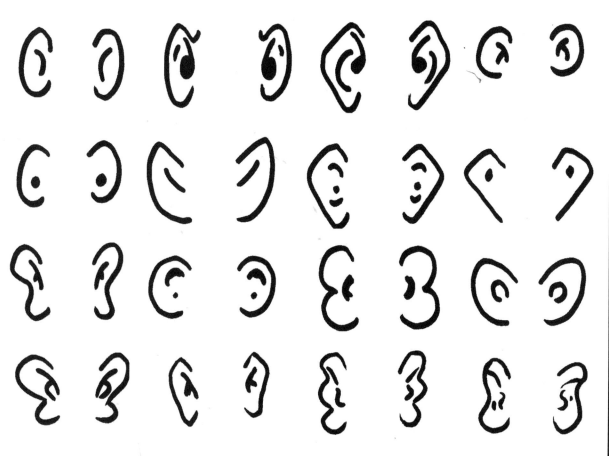

*You have a choice of making the features on your characters complex or simple. Superheroes often have complex features. Many successful characters have simple features. There are no wrong answers. **You** are in charge of the looks of your character!*

HEAD ACCESSORIES!

*The details you put on your characters' faces can tell a lot about them,
where they live, what they do, and sometimes even if they are heroes or villains!*

Glasses

Facial Hair

Ouch!

Make a
Baseball
cap!

Jewelry/Hair Accessories

Hats

CARTOON BODY GESTURES
OR
DRAWING THE HUMAN FIGURE

Gestures are poses. This section contains two different methods of gesture drawing. These are the rounded shape or 'bean' method and the skeleton or 'stick figure' method. For those who are less experienced in cartooning, the bean method may seem easier. Both methods work well and variations of both methods have been used by professional cartoonists for generations.

TIPS ON DRAWING BODIES:

1. Start your drawing using *LIGHT* pencil lines. You will need to erase these lines, so do not press hard with your pencil.

2. Match the expression on the face with the gesture of your character. A happy face and a droopy body may confuse your reader.

3. Pick a pose from the example pages that is close to the pose you want to use and then modify it to suit your needs. Don't hesitate to change arm positions, leg positions, head directions or even body size and shape.

4. Remember all of the bodies in this section can also be used for cartoon animals and other characters that stand up and walk around like humans. This is called **anthropomorphic**. See pages 62-64.

Below are a few examples of the same body pose used for very different characters.
The gesture drawing (stick figure) for these poses is found on page 33. Check it out!

Turn the page and get started drawing some cool cartoon bodies!

GESTURE DRAWING WITH 'BEAN' SHAPES

It's easy and fun to make your characters' bodies active.
Get them on the move starting with an action line.

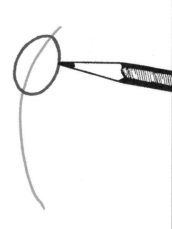

1.

Draw an 'action line' with a *light* pencil line. It will show the direction your character is moving.

Use *light* pencil lines!

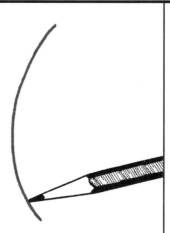

2.

Add the head at the top of the 'action line'.

3.

Add an oval or 'bean' shape under the head for the chest and stomach.

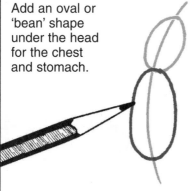

4.

A few curved lines will work very well for the legs. A couple of ovals make the feet.

5.

Curved lines and a couple of circles will give arms and hands a place to live. Bend the elbows and knees for a natural pose.

6.

Ink your character with a black pen. Put the details in and erase your *light* pencil lines.

POSES YOU CAN COPY

Many pros always draw an action line first. Put the circles and ovals on it to create some wonderful poses for your characters. Remember to use light pencil lines so you can easily erase them after you ink your character.

FOUR IMPORTANT POSES AND MORE

Standing

Walking

Jogging

Running

A dark shadow under your character is a good idea.

DETAILS MAKE THE DIFFERENCE!

*The body gesture you use will tell what the character is **doing** but **not** necessarily what your character **looks** like. The costumes and other details you put on the body make a huge difference.*

This gesture drawing makes these characters!

This gesture drawing makes these characters!

TURNAROUND

Turnarounds are drawings of your character from different angles.
Drawing these will eliminate future guesswork about how your character is constructed.

MODEL SHEET

"YOUNG LUMBERJACK" MODEL SHEET 1
School Mascot of Phillips Middle School, Phillips, Wisconsin

Pick a few favorite poses of your character and draw them on a single sheet of paper. You now have a **model sheet!**

These handy movements can make composing a cartoon much easier. Always compare your character with the model sheet. You want your drawing to be **on-model**. That means, looking like the model sheet.

Cartoonists measure a character's height by the number of heads tall it is. Many children are three heads tall and normal adults are five to six heads tall. Superheroes are often eight heads tall.

DRAWING BODIES USING STICK FIGURE GESTURES

If you like to draw superheros, you'll need to start with a good stick figure and then put muscles on it. This is how the pros do it. Stick figures will work for super males, and females – also space aliens, robots and anthropomorphic animals that stand like humans!

DIFFICULTY LEVEL

1.

Start with a *light* action line and add a head shape.

2.

The torso is made up of an oval for the chest and hips and a U-shape for the rib cage.

3.

Arms and legs are lines with circles for joints.

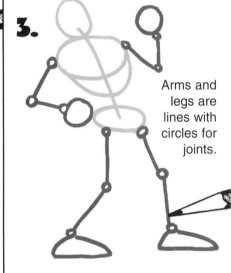

Below are two ways to add muscles to your character.

4A.

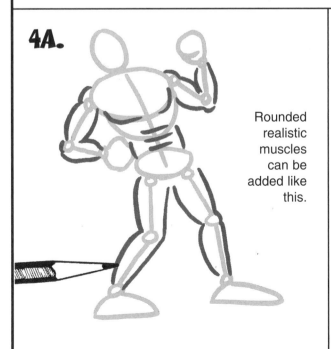

Rounded realistic muscles can be added like this.

4B.

The muscles may also be drawn as cylinders.

GESTURE IDEAS!

Draw these stick figure gestures a few times and then change the position of the arms and legs to make your own poses.

Check out the
action lines
on this page!!
Sketch *lightly*
in pencil then add
muscles and costumes
to create your own
unique characters.

CHARACTER IDEAS!

Many characters can be made from the same gesture drawing. Make up your own characters using this stick figure.

SUPERHERO POSES

Notice how the shoulders and chests are drawn bigger in these stick figures.

Check out comic books or TV shows for more action poses.

DRAWING CARTOON HANDS

The hand is complex because it has so many joints. Drawing it successfully takes practice. Here is an exercise to help you get started drawing hands.

Don't forget.
Light pencil, please!

1. Start with a circle. This is the palm.

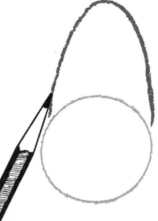

2. Add a shovel shape for the finger area.

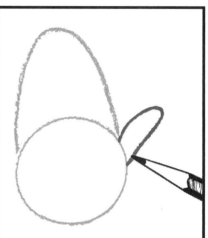

3. Add a thumb on either either side.

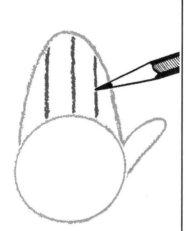

4. Now draw three lines to separate the fingers.

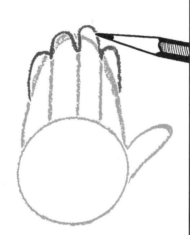

5. Round off the fingertips, like this.

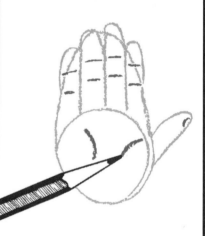

6. Add lines on the palm to show the wrinkles.

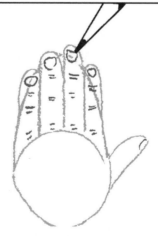

7. The top side of the hand might want finger nails.

8. Trace the lines you want to save with your black pen and erase the *light* pencil lines.

DRAWING ANGLED CARTOON HANDS

Your characters won't always have their hands up straight.
Here is a method you can use to tilt the hands that you draw.

To draw hands flat, like this, use a round shape for the palm.

But when the hand tips and turns, the shape becomes an oval and the fingers will overlap.

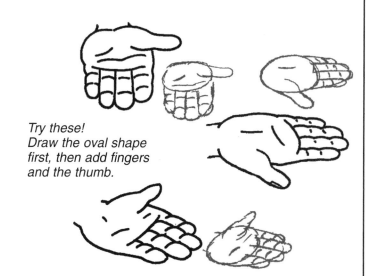

Try these!
Draw the oval shape first, then add fingers and the thumb.

DRAW A FIST OR HAND HOLDING SOMETHING

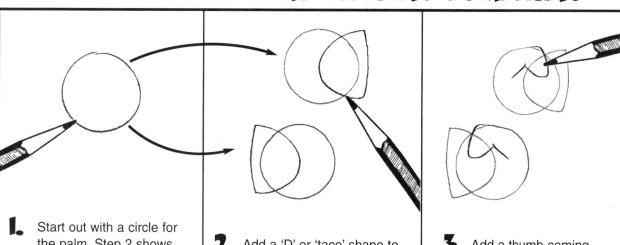

1. Start out with a circle for the palm. Step 2 shows both right and left hand.

2. Add a 'D' or 'taco' shape to either side.

3. Add a thumb coming down over the 'taco'.

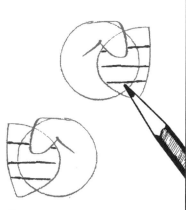

4. Draw three lines to make four fingers.

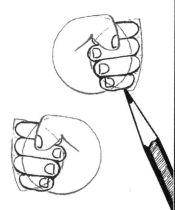

5. Round off the fingers, like this. Add nails.

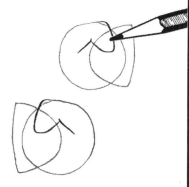

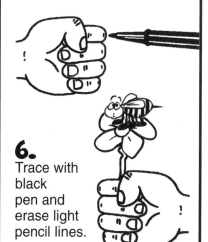

6.
Trace with black pen and erase light pencil lines.

DIFFICULTY LEVEL

IDEAS FOR HAND POSITIONS

Practice drawing these shapes and you'll master hands in no time flat!

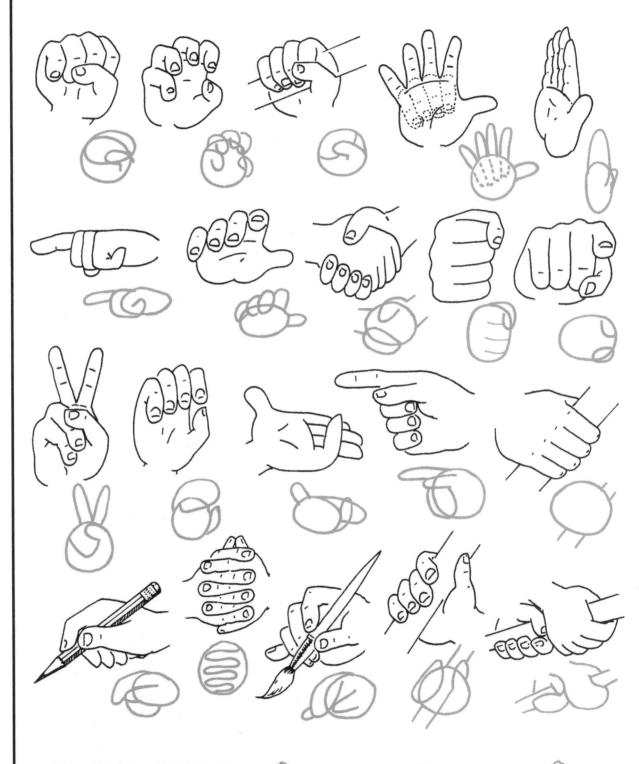

HOW MANY FINGERS?

Three or four fingers, the technique for making hands is still the same.

Use three lines to create four fingers, or two lines to create three fingers.

DRAWING CARTOON FEET!

If your character is out for a day at the beach, you'll need to kick off those shoes! EASY and FUN!

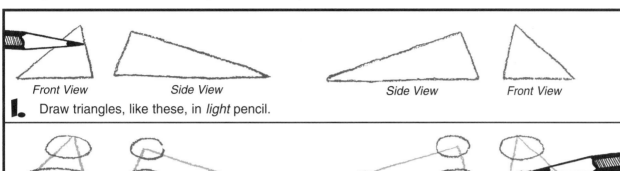

Front View   *Side View*   *Side View*   *Front View*

1. Draw triangles, like these, in *light* pencil.

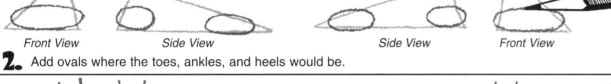

Front View   *Side View*   *Side View*   *Front View*

2. Add ovals where the toes, ankles, and heels would be.

3. Draw gently curved lines to connect the ovals. It's starting to look like a foot!

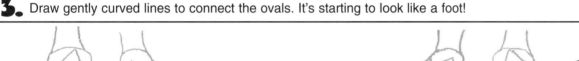

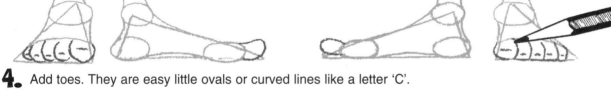

4. Add toes. They are easy little ovals or curved lines like a letter 'C'.

5. Trace in ink and erase all of your *light* pencil lines. OK, now we're ready to run in the sand!

6.

More ideas for feet.

Look at your own shoes for more ideas.

HUMANS ARE FUN! NOW LET'S DRAW CARTOON ANIMALS!

A GOOD PLACE TO START DRAWING ANIMALS IS NONE OTHER THAN. . .

THE DOG!!

Z SNORT

BRUTUS

DANGER

LET'S DRAW A DOG!

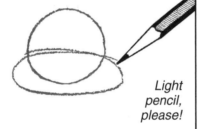

Light pencil, please!

1. The dog is a creature of **shapes**. We'll start with overlapping a circle and an oval.

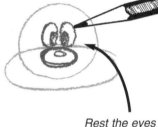

Rest the eyes on this line.

2. The eyes and nose are simple ovals. You can make the dog's nose black when you ink.

3. The mouth is made by drawing the letter 'U' twice side by side. Another big 'U' makes the tongue. Ovals for ears.

By connecting the two circles you have created a 'bean' shape.

4. Add two circles for chest and back end and connect them with some gently curved lines for back and tummy.

The famous cartoon dog, *Pluto,* first appeared in a movie in 1930 called "The Chain Gang". After this, he was called 'Rover' and belonged to Minnie Mouse. Later, he was renamed in honor of the newly discovered planet.

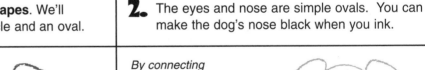

40

5. Curved lines and ovals are all you need to create legs and paws for your dog. Step Six shows you how to add two more legs by *overlapping* the same shapes.

6. Add a shaggy tail and shaggy fur, toes and maybe even a collar. This is the fun part. You're adding the details! OK, let's ink!

Small, light lines show motion.

Add a background. Use your imagination. Where is your dog? What's he doing?

Don't forget to add the doggie slobber!

7. Trace over the lines you want to keep with your black pen. Add a background. Erase the pencil lines.

BY DRAWING THIS DOG, YOU HAVE LEARNED THE **BASIC TECHNIQUE** USED FOR DRAWING MOST CARTOON ANIMALS. **CIRCLES** AND **OVALS**, CONNECTED WITH **CURVED LINES** WILL CREATE JUST ABOUT ANY CARTOON ANIMAL THAT YOU WANT TO DRAW. 'TOON ON!

Dogs are cool! They come in so many sizes and shapes. Turn the page for a few ideas for drawing different kinds of dogs.

IDEAS FOR CREATING DOGS

How large your drawing is depends on the size of the circles and ovals you make!

SNIFF SNIFF SNIFF

Remember, when inking your 'toon, *ink ONLY the lines you want to keep!* Some pencil lines are only for placement and should not become a permanent part of your drawing!

BAD DOG!

43

DRAWING A CARTOON CAT

WOW! THE DOG WAS SO EASY TO DRAW- LET'S DRAW HIS VERY BEST FRIEND...

THE BLACK-CAPPED CHICKADEE?

NO! THE CAT.

GIVE ME A BREAK!

Light pencil, please!

1. We start again with a circle and an oval. We'll overlap them as we did with the dog.

I'M STARTING TO LOOK LIKE A *BIRD!*

2. Add eyes on the top of the overlapping oval and then add a triangle for the nose.

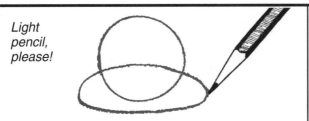

THAT'S BETTER!

3. Use the letter 'U' three times to create the cat's smiling mouth. Add the cat's ears and a skinny neck.

There's that 'bean' shape again!

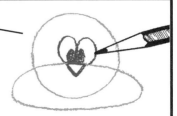

4. Follow steps 4 and 5 in *drawing the dog* (pages 40-41) for the cat's body. Next, add a cat's tail like this.

5. Add the details - **fur, whiskers,** and **more!**

Whiskers? Yup!

Eyebrows, eye lashes, eye lids? Why not!

Add a chin!

Don't forget the kitty's toes and claws!

Random scribbles make great fur. Try this technique for grass, too!

5. OK, get your ink pen, we're ready to add the final details.

Put your cat in an identifiable place.

Trace over your light pencil lines with your black pen and erase all your pencil lines.

Leave a little white spot in each eye pupil. This is a technique used by many professional cartoonists.

Add extras. Maybe a mouse, a bowl of food, a ball of yarn or. . . ?!?!

WHAT A GREAT LOOKING CAT!

IDEAS FOR CATS AND CAT POSES

When heads are slightly turned <u>or</u> you are showing a profile view, see how these ovals move to the side.

CATNIP

45

IDEAS FOR MORE CATS

Use a large circle and a small oval to make a kitten head.

Make a small body and big feet for younger animals.

Add markings on your cats and other animals like stripes or spots.

LET'S DRAW A HORSE.

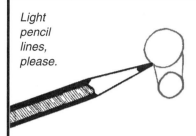

LET'S SEE HOW EASY IT IS TO DRAW ANOTHER ONE OF OUR FOUR-LEGGED FRIENDS.

A CARD TABLE?

NO, SILLY... A HORSE!

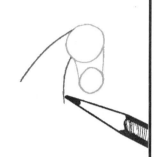

Light pencil lines, please.

1. Start with the head. Two circles - one larger, one smaller - connected with two lines.

2. Add a strong horse neck with curved lines.

DIFFICULTY LEVEL

3. Draw the body the same way you did for the dog and cat with circles and curved lines.

4. Add the legs. Back legs have a curved shape. Use circles for the knees and ankles.

5. Rough in the final details like the mane, tail, and, yes, a cartoon horse can have an expression.

6. Trace with your black pen and erase all of your pencil lines. Don't forget to add a background. Could your horse be in the desert, in school, at the circus or where? You decide.

SEE PAGE 67 FOR MORE BACKGROUNDS.

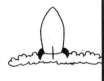

LET'S DRAW A WACKO CARTOON HORSE

1. Start out with a small circle and a large oval. The oval is the *big nose!*

2. Connect the circle and the oval and add a skinny neck.

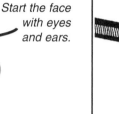

Start the face with eyes and ears.

3. Draw a small circle for the chest and a large circle for the horse back end.

Give your wacky horse a big lip!

4. Connect the circles with curved lines and add mouth and nostrils.

5. Add straight lines for legs. No knees or ankles on a wacky horse!

6. Add very large horse hooves. Hoof shapes overlap one another.

7. Give your horse a mane and tail that show a bad hair day!

8. Ink and give your horse a place to live.

Erase away light pencil lines.

WELL, WE'VE DISCOVERED THAT ANY ANIMAL CHARACTER CAN BE DRAWN USING CIRCLES, OVALS, AND CURVED LINES.

I THOUGHT WE USED A PENCIL!

IF WE WERE AROUND MANY THOUSANDS OF YEARS AGO WE'D BE USING CIRCLES, OVALS AND CURVES TO DRAW DINOSAURS!

NICE COSTUME!

DRAWING DINOSAURS

Draw the shapes lightly with your pencil and then ink your drawings. Put in the details you want and give your dino a place to live.

IDEAS FOR DRAWING MORE DINOS

Cartoons can span space and time!

OH, BABY!

IDEAS FOR DRAWING EVEN MORE DINOS

LET'S DRAW BIRDS AND FISH

The different types of animals you can make by joining circles and ovals together with simple curved lines goes on and on!

I'M SO COOL!

IDEAS FOR MORE BIRDS & FISH

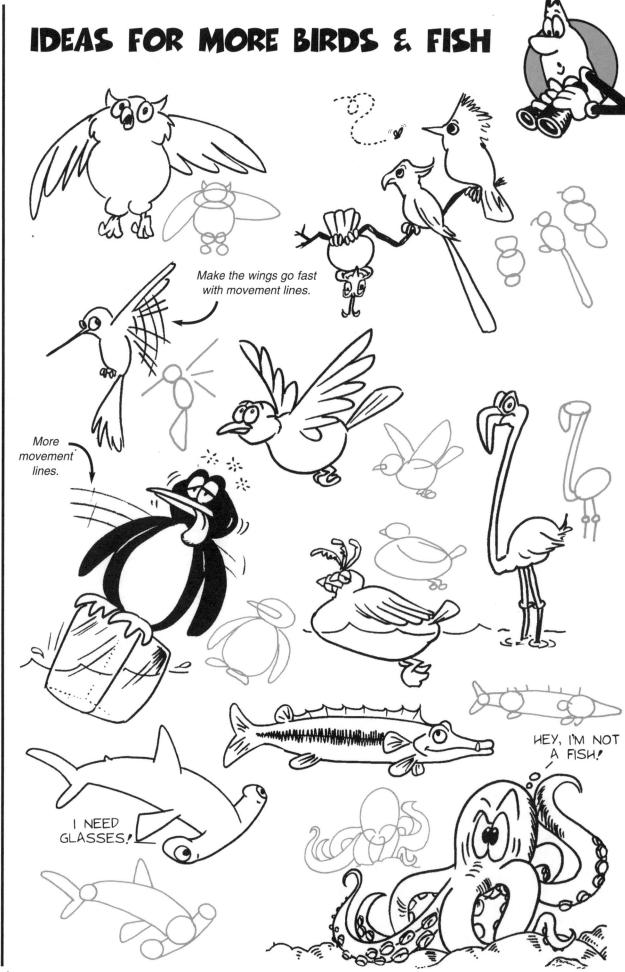

Make the wings go fast with movement lines.

More movement lines.

I NEED GLASSES!

HEY, I'M NOT A FISH!

GET WILD
WITH WILD
ANIMALS

MORE WILD ANIMAL IDEAS!

Cartoon animals are everywhere!
*With **practice**, any animal can be drawn*
with circles, ovals and curves.

Make a
racing
turtle!

LOOK AT ME
JUMPING!

BUGS AND OTHER CRAWLIES

They creep! They crawl! They are cool cartoon characters!

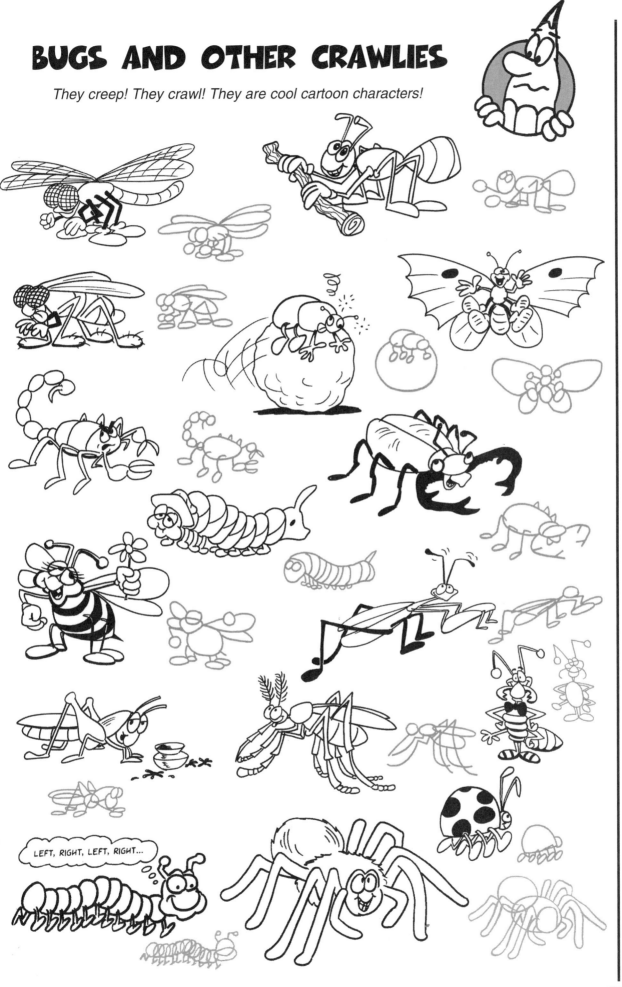

LEFT, RIGHT, LEFT, RIGHT...

ANIMALS DOWN ON THE FARM!

DRAW THESE FUNNY MONSTERS!

It's a good idea to name your characters and give them a personality.

"Loverboy"

"Krankall"

"Fashion Freak"

"Unibrow"

"Pledgedrive"

"Hootenanny"

"Sir Smilzalot"

SPACE ALIENS, ROBOTS & MORE!

*Nobody knows what a real space alien looks like so here
is a great place for you to let your imagination go wild!*

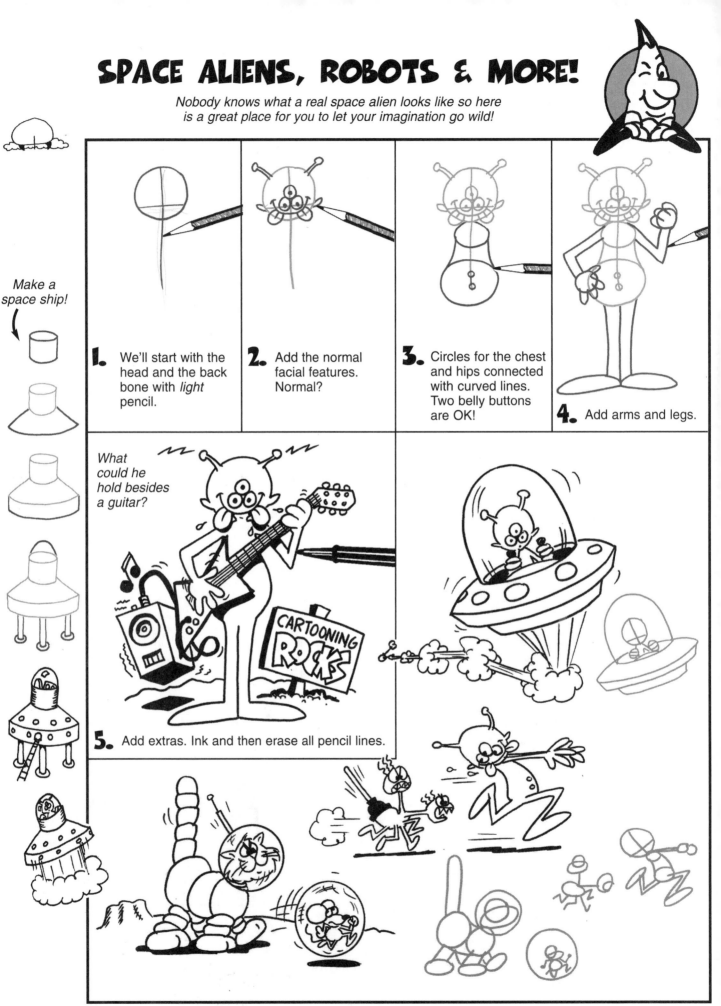

**Make a
space ship!**

1. We'll start with the head and the back bone with *light* pencil.

2. Add the normal facial features. Normal?

3. Circles for the chest and hips connected with curved lines. Two belly buttons are OK!

4. Add arms and legs.

What could he hold besides a guitar?

CARTOONING ROCKS

5. Add extras. Ink and then erase all pencil lines.

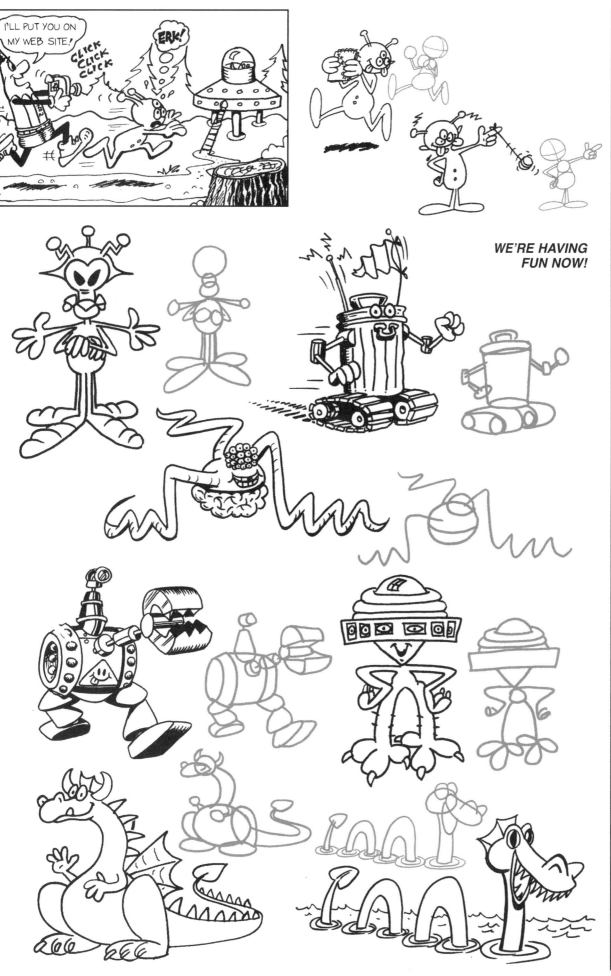

WE'RE HAVING
FUN NOW!

WOW!

I NEVER REALIZED THERE WERE SO MANY DIFFERENT KINDS OF CHARACTERS

IT SEEMS WE'VE SKIPPED ABOUT A ZILLION!

OK - WE'VE CREATED CARTOON **PEOPLE** AND **ANIMALS** AND **MONSTERS** AND **MYTHICAL CREATURES** --THAT JUST ABOUT DOES IT FOR CHARACTERS.

OH, YEAH? WHAT ABOUT YOU? YOU'RE NOT ANY OF THOSE CHARACTERS.

OOPS!

HOW ABOUT MAKING **OBJECTS** INTO CARTOON CHARACTERS?

GREAT IDEA!

SINCE THE EARLIEST DAYS OF CARTOONING, **OBJECTS** HAVE COME TO LIFE. AND, JUST LIKE HUMANS AND ANIMALS AND OTHER CHARACTERS, OBJECTS ARE MADE UP OF SIMPLE SHAPES.

These shapes are used to create many cartoon characters.

CIRCLE   TRIANGLE

OVAL   FREE FORM

SQUARE/RECTANGLE   MANY-SIDED SHAPES

DIFFICULTY LEVEL

To give your cartoons real life, you'll want objects with depth, height and width or **dimension**. This technique is called three-dimensional, or 3-D!

THE CUBE

Let's start with a cube, the building block of many objects used in cartoons! It's easy!

1. Draw two diamond shapes one directly below the other.

2. Connect them with lines from the points.

3. Erase the inside lines, like this.

THE CYLINDER

Many objects start with a basic cylinder shape. It's easy!

1. Draw two oval shapes one directly below the other.

2. Connect the ovals with two straight lines.

3. Erase the top of the bottom oval, like this.

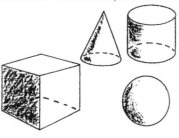

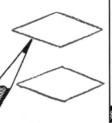

THE CONE

A cone is just an upside down 'V' sitting on top of an oval.

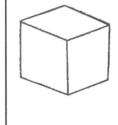

THE SPHERE

A sphere is a circle with shading on one side.

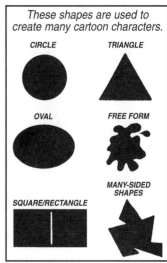

ANTHROPOMORPHIC CHARACTERS!

ANTHROPOMORPHIC IS ONE **BIG** WORD!

HMMM... ANTHROPOMORPHIC... TO CHANGE SOMETHING INTO SOMETHING HUMAN-LIKE. JUST LIKE YOU, NO. 2.

NO. 2?... NO. 2?

HEY, WHERE DID HE GO? ?!?

I HAVE AN IDEA! LET'S...

DRAW HIM!!

DIFFICULTY LEVEL

1. Draw a tall cylinder.

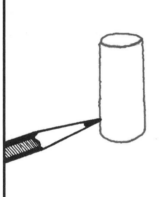

2. Add a cone shape.

Draw a wavy lead line.

CONEHEAD, HA, HA!

3. Draw two lines for the flat sides of his body.

Add curved lines for the eraser.

Cylinders are good for drawing all sorts of things, from a hockey puck, a spool of thread, or a truck tire. They are the best thing to know how to draw, right No. 2?

4. Add an expression and more details.

RIGHT!

These lines are the letter 'U' upside down.

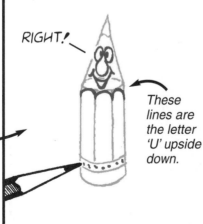

5. Add the arms, legs, hands and feet.

6. Add the details. Trace with your black pen and erase pencil lines.

I'M BACK!

NO. 2

64

ONE-POINT PERSPECTIVE

Perspective drawing will help you show distance and depth in your cartoons.

1. Start with a horizontal line like this.
This is the HORIZON.

Light pencil!

A dot on the horizon line becomes the VANISHING POINT (the place that is so far away you can't see it anymore).

2. Now draw a few straight lines from the vanishing point.

You can use a ruler if you like.

3. Next draw horizontal and vertical lines. You can make rectangles touching your existing lines. A few more horizontal and vertical lines will make CUBES.

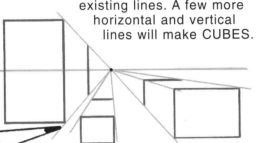

4. More cubes could make a city.

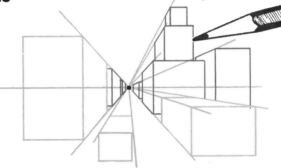

5. Trace only the lines you want to keep in black ink and erase all of the guidelines.

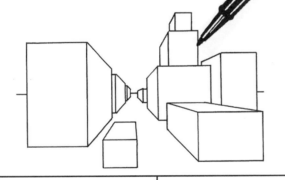

It may take a while to master perspective.
Don't give up!
With practice you will soon have the whole world in perspective!

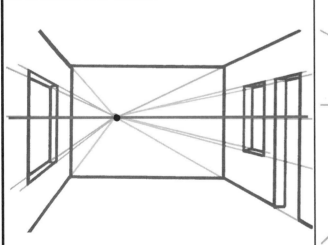

One-point perspective will help you draw interiors of buildings. Your characters should have a place to live, work or go to school.

Use your imagination and you will discover many uses for one point perspective.

TWO-POINT PERSPECTIVE

When you want to view an object from a corner and see more than one side, then two-point perspective is the technique that will do the job.
For best results, use a ruler or other straight edge for all straight lines.

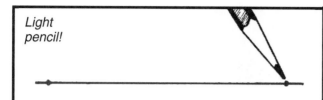

DIFFICULTY LEVEL

Light pencil!

You may use a ruler or straight edge.

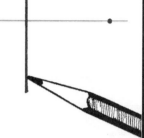

1. Start by drawing a horizontal line (your horizon) and put two dots on it. These dots are vanishing points. Usually these are spaced near each end of the horizon line.

2. Draw a vertical line crossing anywhere between the two vanishing points.

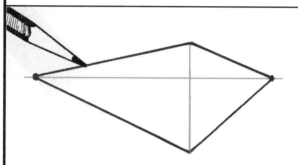

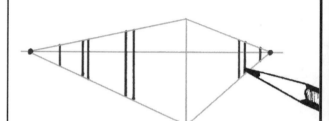

3. Draw light lines from your vertical line to the vanishing points like this.

4. Add more vertical lines to define the edges of cubes. Add more lines for more shapes.

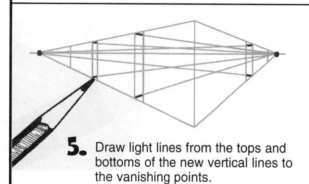

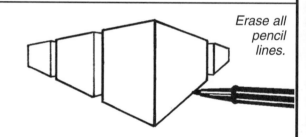

Erase all pencil lines.

5. Draw light lines from the tops and bottoms of the new vertical lines to the vanishing points.

6. Trace over the pencil lines of the objects you want to keep with black ink.

IDEAS

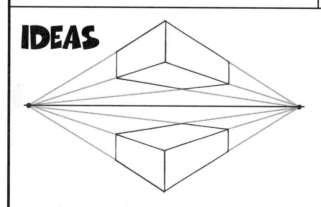

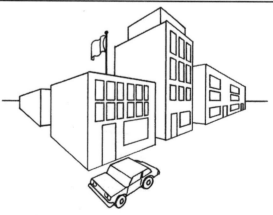

If you want to see three sides of an object, draw it completely above or below the horizon line.

With practice, you will easily see how drawing a complex scene like this becomes a matter of one horizon line and two vanishing points.

BACKGROUND IDEAS

Your characters should appear in an identifiable place. Try these, then create more of your own scenes. Look in comic strips and comic books to see more examples of backgrounds.

SINGLE PANEL CARTOONS!

Single panel cartoons have <u>one</u> drawing that tells the cartoon story.

Here are the steps in drawing a single panel cartoon. You will need an **idea**, **characters** and a **setting**.

Helpful tips are found on the following pages:

Character Ideas – Pages 6-64
Getting Ideas – Page 72
Background Ideas – Page 67
Cartoon Symbols – Page 73

Sketch out several of your ideas in small pictures. These are called **thumbnail sketches.** Next, choose the best thumbnail sketch and draw it bigger as shown in step 1.

DIFFICULTY LEVEL

TIP! Most professional cartoonists write very clearly in capital letters so the words they write can be read.

1. Sketch your cartoon idea on a plain sheet of white paper in *light pencil.* Draw light guidelines for your lettering.

2. Trace your drawing in black ink starting with the lettering. Erase all of the pencil lines. Sign your cartoon *inside* the panel.

3. Black areas in your cartoons will add contrast and focus, and they will look a lot better, too!

See symbols on page 73 for examples of *stippling* and *cross-hatching.*

4A. Add gray areas by cross hatching or stippling in black ink. *OR...*

4B. ...if you have a computer, a scanner and graphics software, add gray tones or color.

SINGLE PANEL CARTOON EXAMPLES!

Many of these ideas came from page 72.

"I'LL BE A LITTLE LATE... I'M STUCK IN TRAFFIC."

"I CLEANED MY ROOM, JUST DON'T LOOK IN THE CLOSET."

NEWLY WASHED CARS
BALD HEADS

"NOW LET'S MOVE ON TO **SECONDARY** TARGETS..."

GARBAGE

"DON'T FIX SUPPER. I'LL PICK UP SOMETHING ON THE WAY HOME"

"TRICK OR TREAT!"

THE MAKEOVER SHOW

"HUMPTY DUMPTY...YOU'VE BEEN CHOSEN FOR OUR MAKEOVER SHOW!!"

MULTI-PANEL COMIC STRIPS

Multi-panel cartoons (comic strips) are drawn with two or more pictures. The drawings in the frames (panels) of the comic are placed next to each other to form a **strip**; *that's how we get the term* **comic strip!** *Comic strips are stories with pictures. They have a...*

...BEGINNING, →	...MIDDLE,		and END
Draw the start of a story or joke in the first panel.	*Draw the middle of your story or joke in the next panel.*	*Add more panels if you need them.*	*Draw the conclusion (or punch line) of your story or joke in the last panel.*

Here are two techniques for creating comic strips:

JOKE TECHNIQUE

This is an example of simply taking a joke and having your characters tell the joke. The lettering always reads from left to right and top to bottom. Here, the lettering was done first and the characters were drawn after the lettering. The steps in drawing these comic strips are the same as were used on page 68. Now try one of your jokes!

SIGHT GAG TECHNIQUE

A **sight gag** is a cartoon that you need to see to understand. The joke above would still be funny without the drawing. You must see the pictures in a sight gag to understand the humor. The example below uses a *loud noise* (**onomatopoeia***) and a *surprise ending*. Here the flower looses it's petals after a sneeze.

What would happen if a porcupine sneezed, or a bird, or a really hairy dog? Add your characters and see how easy it is to make a multi-panel, onomatopoeia comic strip.

*An **onomatopoeia** is a word that imitates a sound or action. **WHOOSH, BANG, ZOOM,** and **KERPLUNK** are examples of onomatopoeia words.

MORE COMIC STRIP EXAMPLES

Use your imagination, jokes, and make up sounds for some really cool comic strips!

TIP! Use a ruler or other straight edge for all of your straight lines.

LETTERING, ONOMATOPOEIA, & DIALOGUE BALLOONS

Look for more examples in the Sunday paper comic section.

Outline

Solid

Overlap

Connected

Block

Drop Shadow

TIP! Always sign your name *inside* of one of the panels. Make it artistic, but readable!

HERE IS A GOOD WAY TO GET IDEAS FOR YOUR CARTOONS

Think about your character(s) in many different situations.
Ask yourself questions to get your brain moving.

Mix and match characters and situations!

You'll find funny and unique combinations. Go ahead and laugh out loud!

Think to yourself ***"What if . . . ?"***

Ask yourself questions about the characters or the situations.

"If I was a space alien, (bear, wrestler, etc.) what movie, (club, activity, etc.) would interest me?"

Make up silly questions to ask your character and think of silly answers they might give you. Draw the great cartoon ideas that pop into your head!!

Have fun!

Keep adding to these lists. Keep a journal or a sketch book of funny things you see that are amusing or unusual. The possibilities are endless and only limited by your own imagination!

Characters & Situations

Characters	Situations
Deer	Reading a newspaper
Alligator	Driving a truck
Moose	Ironing clothes
Sharks	Discovering a buried _____.
Sports dude	Cleaning a Room
Bears	Painting a picture or a house
Fly	Watching TV
Cat	Hiding
Bird	Talking on a cell phone
Spider	Eating
Scientist	Conducting a science experiment
Little kid	Reading a book
Lamb	Eating a _____ pizza
Apes	Going trick or treating
Wolves	Getting a drink at a drinking fountain
Dog	Looking out of a window at _____.
Snakes	Playing a video game
Cave people	Being awakened by a _____.
Ancient Egyptians	Digging a hole to put a _____ in it.
Dr. Frankenstein	Working on an assembly line
One cell animals	Playing a trick on _____.
Monsters	Singing Happy Birthday to _____.
Dinosaurs	Watching _____ move in next door.
Horse	Doing aerobics
Doctor	Charging across a moat
Space creatures	Talking around a campfire
Elephants	Cutting something with a saw or knife
Farmer	Going to a museum/zoo/movies/amusement park
Teacher	Swinging from a tree
Cow	Sitting in a chair
Chicken	Looking in an aquarium
Baby	Playing baseball
Sled Dogs	Driving a tractor
Skeleton	Playing music on a _____.
Jungle person	Eating bananas
Pirate	Explaining something at a blackboard
Psychiatrist	In a radioactive area
Humpty Dumpty	Going on a date
Whales	Cutting down a tree
Octopus	Getting mail
Cowboy	Playing a piano
Turtle	Dreaming
Mouse	Playing with a balloon
Man-eating plant	Working on a computer
Worm	Singing in an opera

COOL CARTOON SYMBOLS FOR YOUR CARTOONS!

Here are a few ideas for making your cartoons come to life.
Show movement, wind, gravity, speed and a whole lot more with symbols.

Stippling for shading

Hatch and Cross Hatch for shading ➝

LET'S MAKE A
TWO-PART ANIMATION!

Cartoon animation on television and movies is created by showing thousands of images very rapidly. You can make your own animation with just two drawings. It's easy and fun to do.

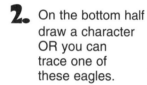

Go to page 55 to see the shapes you need to draw this eagle.

1. Fold a sheet of plain white paper in half and open it up again.

2. On the bottom half draw a character OR you can trace one of these eagles.

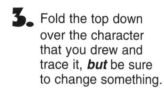

3. Fold the top down over the character that you drew and trace it, *but* be sure to change something.

4. Now flip the top of the paper rapidly and see how the character appears to be move! You have just created an animation!

Wouldn't a two-part animation make a great greeting card?

IDEAS FOR 2-PART ANIMATION

Here are a few ideas for making your cartoons come to life.
Show movement, wind, gravity, speed with the symbols shown on page 73.
You can make a two-part animation out of any of the characters in this book!

MAKE AN ANIMATION FLIP BOOK!

Flip books have been around for over 100 years.
Have fun making your own with a tablet of paper and a pencil or pen.

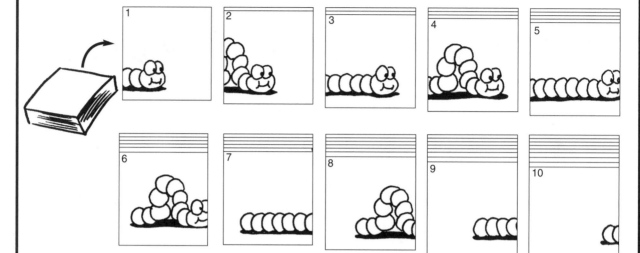

Making a flip book using sticky notes

1. Peel off the top sheet and stick it to your drawing surface.

2. Print a small number '1' on the upper corner and draw your first drawing on the paper. Use a dark pencil or dark pen so you can see it through the next sheet.

3. Take another sheet and stick it *slightly lower* than the first sheet. Number it and draw your next image.

4. Repeat the process until the animation is finished.

5. Add a little color with colored pencils and you are ready to bring your animation to life.

6. Now hold the stack of drawings in one hand and flip them from back to front with the other thumb like this. ⟶

7. Share your flip book with friends and try more animations.

Other ideas:

You can make flip books with a tablet of unlined paper. Start from the back and draw your animation on each sheet as in the sticky note exercise. Another way to create a flip book is to draw on index or recipe cards and bind the pack of cards together at one end with rubber bands. Be sure to number all of your drawings in case they get out of order.

Copy or trace the drawings on this page, use the animations in the margins of this book or create your own action-packed animations!

ANIMATE A WALKING HORSE

1   2   3

4   5   6

7   8   9

IN CONCLUSION...

We hope you have enjoyed Cartooning Basics. It's been fun writing and illustrating this book and we have done our best to make it fun, entertaining, and educational. We hope you have as much fun cartooning as we do! Happy 'tooning!   *DUANE AND ANGIE BARNHART*

NO. 2's TOP TEN 'TOON TIPS

1. BE PREPARED. Have your materials handy. You don't want to run out of paper or sharp pencils when the mood to 'toon strikes.

2. LEARN FROM THE PRO'S. Look at cartoon strips and cartoon books created by artists who really know how to draw and how to make their stories interesting. Don't follow the crowd with the latest fad cartoon unless it is well done.

3. USE THE LIBRARY! Libraries have zillions of ideas. Find time to "surf the shelves" for pictures and ideas.

4. VISIT CARTOON EXHIBITS, MUSEUMS, AND STUDIOS. Examine original art drawn by cartoon masters just as any other artist would examine the artwork of the masters of fine art.

5. COPY YOUR CARTOONS AND SHARE THEM WITH FRIENDS AND FAMILY. Keep your original cartoons in a safe place, stored flat, not folded or rolled. If you save your original drawings, you can always make copies to share on the copy machine at the library.

6. DON'T USE OTHER CARTOONISTS' CHARACTERS AND CALL THEM YOUR OWN. It is not only illegal, it robs *you* of the satisfaction of creating your own characters and can prove to be embarrassing.

7. MAKE A MORGUE. A morgue is a collection of pictures clipped from magazines and such as *people, costumes, scenery, animals*, or *whatever* interests you. The internet is also a great resource for reference material.

8. PRACTICE EVERY DAY. It is easy to get busy and not have time to draw. But just as in sports, if you don't practice, your skills slip away. A few minutes of drawing each day will improve your skills and keep them sharp. Soon you'll look forward to your daily 'toon time.

9. DRAW AND REDRAW YOUR CARTOONS. Redraw it until you get it the way you want it. If you are trying something difficult, have patience and confidence that you'll get it the way you want it if you practice.

10. TAKE CLASSES IN CARTOONING AND RELATED FIELDS. Some communities don't have cartooning instructors, so take classes in drawing and writing. Some cartoonists actually take acting and clowning classes so they can learn to pose their characters better. Support local arts organizations and encourage them to sponsor cartooning classes.

HAPPY 'TOONING!

GLOSSARY

Action Line
An invisible line following the backbone of characters which shows direction and movement.

Advertising Cartoon
A cartoon that is used to sell a product or service.

Animation
Many drawings shown rapidly giving the illusion of movement.

Anthropomorphic
A non-human object/animal which acts like a human.

Background
The environment where cartoon characters appear.

Balloon
An area where the words and thoughts of cartoon characters are written.

Body Expression
The same as gesture drawing. Showing what the cartoon character is doing.

Cartoon
A simple drawing, often makes us laugh by telling a funny story.

Cartooning Basics
Beginning cartooning skills. Also the name of this book.

Cartooning pen
A black ink pen used to finalize cartoons. It doesn't smudge after it's dry.

Cartoonist
A person who loves to draw cartoons, like you!

Characters
The 'actors' in cartoons.

Circle
A very round shape. A very important shape in cartoons.

Comic Book
A small book which tells a story using cartoons.

Comic Strip
A cartoon which appears in newspapers or magazines regularly.

Cone
A geometric shape like an ice cream holder.

Copier Paper
Paper used in a copy machine. White is best for cartooning.

Costume
The clothing worn by cartoon characters.

Cross-hatched Lines
Solid intersecting lines which help to show shadow or pattern.

Cube
A geometric shape like a toy block with six equal sides.

Cylinder
A geometric shape formed by connecting two ovals with straight lines.

Editorial Cartoon
A cartoon that makes us think about events that are current topics in the news.

Eraser
A soft piece of rubber which allows erasing pencil lines after cartoons have been traced with a black pen.

Eye Line
The guide line that shows where the eyes will live on a character.

Expression
Showing feelings and emotion.

Facial Expression
Showing feelings and emotion by the look on a character's face.

Flip Book
Many drawings on a tablet that, when flipped through the fingers, show the illusion of movement.

Cartooning pen
A black ink pen used to finalize cartoons. It doesn't smudge after it's dry.

Gesture drawing
Giving action to cartoon characters' bodies by using interesting stick figures or 'bean' shapes.

Guidelines
Erasable pencil lines used for positioning a character's body and parts of the face.

Hatched Lines
Parallel vertical or horizontal lines which show shadow or pattern.

Head
The thinking, seeing, smelling, eating, hearing part of our bodies. Also a unit of measurement for drawing the height of cartoon characters.

Horizon Line
The line in a drawing that shows the angle at which the drawing is viewed (eye level).

Horizontal
A 'laying down line'. It goes from left to right.

Joints
The parts in our bodies that can bend, like elbows, hips, knees, neck, and knuckles.

Light Lines
Touching your pencil to the paper lightly so the lines can be easily erased later after inking.

Loose Lines
Allowing your pencil to draw freely without tension in your hand.

Model Sheet
Drawings which show a character in many poses to be used when creating panel cartoons.

Morgue
An organized box or other container to keep reference pictures for future drawings.

Mugging
Making faces in the mirror so we can draw expressions.

Multi-panel Cartoon
A cartoon strip that has two or more drawing to tell the story.

No. 2
A pencil used in schools. Also the name of the main character this book.

Nose/Mouth Line
The vertical guideline on a character's face which show where to place the nose and mouth.

Number 2
Same as No. 2.

One Point Perspective
Using only one vanishing point on the horizon line to show depth and distance in drawing.

Onomatopoeia
A word which imitates a sound or action, like *buzz* or *thump.*

Oval
A squashed circle.

Overlap
Positioning one shape over another so that one peeks out from behind the other.

Pencil
An essential tool used by cartoonists. Made of wood with a graphite core. Use it everyday to make fun cartoon characters.

'Practice makes perfect!'
An old saying that is as true today as it was when it was first spoken. The more we practice, the more we will succeed.

Professional Cartoonist
An artist who earns money by drawing cartoons. Called a 'pro'.

Profile
A side view. On humans you will only see one ear. See cartoon of the nice lady on this page!

Roughing-in
A technique used to fill in the fat and muscle over the stick figure of a cartoon character.

Shapes
Forms used to create cartoon characters, most often circles, ovals but also other geometric forms.

Single Panel Cartoon
A cartoon that has only one drawing to tell the story.

Stick Figure
The 'skeleton' of a cartoon character. Shows where joints are located.

Stipple
Making close dots with a black drawing pen to show shadow and pattern.

Superhero
An action cartoon character who usually has super powers.

Symbols
Drawing in a cartoon which help to show speed, gravity, wet, cold, movement. feeling and a lot more.

Television
A wonderful, entertainment invention. Should be used in moderation to avoid addiction.

Trace
Copying a drawing by following the lines as seen through a transparent paper. Going over a pencil line with a black pen.

Three-fourths View
Turning the cartoon head so it's seen from an angle.

3/4 view
Same as three-fourths view.

Turnarounds
Drawings showing a character from front, back and sides.

Two Point Perspective
Using two vanishing points on a horizon line. Shows depth and distance in drawing.

Vanishing Point
The point(s) on the horizon line where lines meet when drawing in perspective.

Vertical Line
An 'up and down line' which goes from top to bottom.

Warm-up Exercises
Quickly sketching circles, ovals and curved lines to prepare for cartooning!

79

INDEX

LOOK IT UP!

SSSSUPER!

GREAT BOOKS FOR *INFORMATION* AND *FUN!*

CHECK IT OUT!

BIBLIOGRAPHY

Finch, Christopher, *The Art of Walt Disney: from Mickey Mouse to the Magic Kingdom,* Harry N. Abrams, Incorporated, New York, 1995.

Waugh, Coulton, *The Comics,* University Press of Mississippi, Jackson & London, 1947.

Lee, Stan and Buscema, John, *How to Draw Comics the Marvel Way,* A Fireside Book, Simon & Schuster, Inc., New York, 1984.

Horn, Maurice. (ed.), *The World Encyclopedia of Comics,* Chelsea House Publishers, New York, 1976.

Richardson, John Adkins, *The Complete Book of Cartooning,* Prentice-Hall, Inc., New Jersey, 1977.

Waid, Mark. (intro.), *Superman in Action Comics,* Abbeville Publishing Group, New York, 1993.

Wilson, Marjorie, and Brent Wilson, *Teaching Children to Draw, a Guide for Teachers & Parents,* Prentice-Hall, Inc., New Jersey, 1982.

SUGGESTED READING FOR MORE CARTOON FUN!

Funny Pictures: Cartooning with Charles M. Schulz, by Charles M. Schulz, Peanuts Interactive Books, Published by Harper Collens Juvenile Books, San Francisco.

How to Animate Film Cartoons, by Preston Blair, Walter Foster Publishing, Inc.

How to Draw Animal Cartoons, by Ed Nofziger, Walter Foster Publishing, Inc.

How to Draw Cartoon Animation, by Preston Blair, Walter Foster Publishing, Inc.

How to Draw Cartoon Animation, by Walter Foster, Walter Foster Publishing, Inc.,

How to Draw Comics the Marvel Way, by Stan Lee and John Buscema, A Fireside Book, Published by Simon & Schuster, Inc.

Mark Kistler's Draw Squad, and *Mark Kistler's Imagination Station,* by Mark Kistler, Fireside Books, Published by Simon & Schuster Inc., New York.

PLACES TO SEE CARTOON ART!

Cartoon Art Museum of San Francisco
655 Mission Street, San Francisco, CA 94105
Exhibits work of popular cartoonists and cartoon art.

Charles M. Schulz Museum
2301 Hardies Lane, Santa Rosa CA 95403
Feature the work of Peanuts creator, Charles M. Schulz

Disney World, MGM Studios
Orlando Florida
Observe animators as they produce new creations for Disney Studios.

Gallery Lainzberg
222 Third Street SE, Cedar Rapids, Iowa 52401
America's oldest and largest gallery specializing exclusively in animation art.

LET US KNOW!

We have tried our best to make this book fun and useable for young cartoonists. We invite teachers, parents and other grownups to use cartooning as an introduction to the wonderful world of art. We'd love your input in improving future editions. **Visit our web site for downloadable lessons, school and library visits and lots more.   www.cartooningbasics.com**

Editor's Note: "Cartooning Basics" is a fresh, original approach to the basics of cartooning for children. Any resemblance to ideas, words, or characters (except in the history section) other than our own is unintentional, and purely coincidental.

ORDERING INFORMATION:

Cartooning Basics - Creating the Characters
by Duane and Angie Barnhart
Eighty-eight pages of basic, how-to-get-started, cartooning fun!
Great for home, school and children's organizations.
$12.99 plus shipping.

Cartooning Basics with Duane Barnhart
Draw along with Duane Barnhart using the professional cartooning techniques he shows in his book, *Cartooning Basics-Creating the Characters*. Thirty minutes of fun draw-along lessons.
$19.99 plus shipping.
Video or DVD format *(Please specify format choice.)*

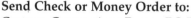

Send Check or Money Order to:
Cartoon Connections Press, PO Box 10889, White Bear Lake, MN 55110
Internet Orders with credit card: www.cartooningbasics.com
Telephone Orders with credit card: 651-429-1244
Shipping: Media Rate. $3.00 for one product and $1.00 for each additional product
Sales Tax: Minnesota residents please add 6.5% sales tax to your order.

Dealer inquiries welcome. Thank You!